Leadership Isn't Rocket Science

Simple Strategies Used by Great Leaders

By

Grant Thompson, Psy.D.

Author photo by Nancy Thompson

ISBN 978-0-9841764-0-3

For additional copies of this book go to
www.thompsonconsulting.com

For my parents, Brenda and Virgil Thompson

Acknowledgments

Thanks to Kathy McIntosh, Vince Morales and my wife, Nancy, for your insights and editing skills.

Table of Contents

Section V: Simple Motivational Strategies

Introduction

"Great leaders are almost always great simplifiers."

- Colin Powell

Corporate America has an amazing ability to make things more complicated than necessary. Company bureaucracy, office politics, and endless meetings are a few of the obstacles to business success. Executives, who are well compensated to develop and communicate a clear vision, often contribute to employee confusion with their business jargon and ever-changing business strategies.

What most leaders fail to understand is that good leadership is simple. Yet corporate America struggles with simplicity. Instead, organizations spend billions of dollars each year searching for the magic formula to cure their organizations' ills. At least once a year, they roll out a trendy new management program guaranteed to motivate employees and maximize profits.

Here's a small sampling of leadership fads in vogue over the years: Team-Based Management, Matrix Management, Management by Objectives (MBO), Total Quality Management (TQM), Inclusive Leadership, and Democratic Consultative Leadership. Whew. You've got to feel sorry for the poor supervisor who needs to refer to a business school textbook just to understand the latest leadership "flavor of the month" being rolled out by company executives.

Don't get me wrong. I am a huge believer in training managers and providing them leadership tools. I guess I'm just more of a meat and potatoes guy when it comes to leading employees. In my job as a management consultant, I have worked with hundreds of companies and observed thousands of managers in action. I have seen supervisors beg, bribe, ask, order, cajole, manipulate, and threaten employees in an effort to improve performance. And now, more than ever, I'm convinced the most effective leaders in corporate America are those who stick to basic leadership concepts.

Simply put, this book is about simplifying the leadership process. The book profiles some great leaders who use timeless, rock solid, ultra simple strategies. I also point out some of the most common leadership blunders and poke fun at those managers who make leadership too complicated or who take themselves too seriously. I interviewed dozens of leaders in preparation for this book including some CEOs and/or presidents of large corporations. However, I also interviewed dozens of individuals from different industries and at different levels in organizations because many of the best leaders are found outside the boardroom.

This book consists of a series of short chapters about different leadership topics. The chapters are independent of one another and can be read in any order depending on your interests. The concepts are relevant to managers at all levels, from executives to first-time supervisors.

If you want to find out about the latest leadership "trend," this book isn't for you. Instead, it is an effort to make managing employees easier. It is about utilizing leadership fundamentals that proved effective 100 years ago, and will be effective a century from now. It is about simplifying the leadership process because leadership isn't rocket science.

Note: All of the scenarios presented in the book actually occurred. However, in some instances, I have altered identifying information (name, job title, company, etc.) to respect confidentiality.

Part I

SIMPLE LEADERSHIP STRATEGIES

Simple Strategy #1

Make People Your Priority

"Get the right people in the right jobs—it's more important than strategy."

-Jack Welch

I once met the owner of a construction company who routinely fired two or three employees before lunch. Arrive a few minutes late, terminated! Make a mistake, gone! Suggest a new approach, canned! When I asked why he was so quick to terminate employees he said, "Why waste my time or the company's money? If someone doesn't fit into our system, I cut our losses and hire another employee."

Was this owner being too black and white? Yes. Will his business succeed in the long term? Based on my experience, it is highly unlikely. He was convinced, however, that workers were disposable and that operations and strategy would ultimately determine the success or failure of his company.

I regularly find myself immersed in the "people versus systems" debate with my consulting clients. I recently had a CEO tell me, "People come and go, but if you've got the right operations in place, you can just plug in new employees." I challenged his premise that systems and strategy were more important than people, but my efforts to persuade him failed. Unfortunately, since our discussion, dozens of talented employees have left his organization, many to the competition.

Count Bob Dyson, the owner of 22 Napa Auto Parts stores throughout the Northwest, among those who believe good employees trump strategy and operations when it comes to determining business success. "I succeed or fail based on my people. It's that simple," says Dyson, who has worked in the parts business for nearly three decades. "Inventory, operations—we've pretty much got that figured out. It's all about finding and retaining good people."

> **"I succeed or fail based on my people. It's that simple."**
> Bob Dyson, Owner
> Napa Auto Parts

In particular, Dyson needs good store managers. "A strong manager with judgment and people skills brings in new customers and keeps me out of sticky employment and personnel issues," he says. "On the other hand, if I get the wrong person in as a manager, he chases off my long-time customers and my good employees. Poor managers also result in lots of human resource problems."

Most of Dyson's stores do about a million dollars annually in sales. So what kind of impact can a talented store manager have on the bottom line? "It can be as much as a 50% increase or decrease in sales over a year's time just based on the quality of the store manager. That's $1.5 million compared to a store doing $500,000. A good manager makes that much difference."

Like Dyson, I believe that business success hinges largely on people. Employee turnover is costly because of the expense to recruit, hire, and train new workers. And if you are turning over your top performers, the costs are immeasurable and will almost certainly lead to the destruction of your company (see Simple Strategy 6).

Your organization can have the greatest business plan and the best technology around, but staff it with a bunch of mediocre employees and you will eventually fail. On the other hand, a strong leader surrounded by talented, hungry employees can make money dozens of different ways.

"I could open 10 stores in the next year if I had the managers to run them," says Dyson. "Selling auto parts is simple. Finding and retaining the right people to run the stores is by far my biggest challenge."

Develop Them or Lose Them

"The wisest mind has something yet to learn."

- George Santayana

George Kotch and his team of scientists at Syngenta Seeds are always striving to produce the next great melon. Whether it's creating a firmer cantaloupe or a sweeter watermelon, Kotch is continually trying to perfect the company's products.

Kotch, who has a Ph.D. in genetics, takes a similar scientific approach to developing employees. He constantly analyzes the people who work for him, identifying strengths and weaknesses, and providing employees with opportunities to improve.

"The most important role I have as a manager is developing employees," says Kotch. "Employees need to keep growing and getting better. Otherwise, they'll get stagnant or even get worse."

Few leaders spend as much time focusing on employee development as Kotch. "We don't have the time," and "It's not in the budget," are common excuses managers make for failing to develop their employees. However, my personal favorite is, "We'll develop these employees and then they'll take their skills to the competition."

If you consistently hear these types of excuses in your company, be very concerned. It's only a matter of time until your top employees begin leaving you.

High performing employees are always looking to improve themselves, and the minute they start feeling stale, they are likely to move on to pursue new challenges. "Most of the people working for me are scientists," says Kotch. "Just making a good living isn't enough to retain my best employees. They want to constantly be learning."

"The most important role I have as a manager is developing employees."

George Kotch, Global Crop Leader
Syngenta Seeds

Unfortunately, some managers are fearful of developing employees because they don't want to someday be replaced by their high performers. These managers are obviously being short-sighted. The best leaders don't get caught up in petty jealousy. They have the confidence to advance themselves and their companies by hiring, training, and mentoring as many talented people as possible.

Here are a few of my suggestions for further developing your high performers:

- **Identify a career path.** Make certain your top employees know they have a bright future with the company. Talk to them about possible career paths and help employees develop written Professional Development Plans outlining career goals.

- **Reimburse tuition.** If one of your employees wants to go to night school, that's good news. So-so managers feel threatened by degree-seeking employees.

Great managers encourage employees to seek more education and support them financially.

- **Make employees entrepreneurs.** Perhaps the best way to keep talented people engaged is to allow them to be entrepreneurs within your company. Assign your top employees challenging projects and give them a great deal of autonomy.

- **Provide initial and ongoing training opportunities.** While technical training is fine (e.g., learning the organization's computer systems), make certain some training focuses on developing the individual for future responsibilities (e.g., leadership skills).

- **Praise employees like crazy.** It never ceases to amaze me how many top employees leave companies having never been told they had bright futures with the organization. They don't receive praise from their supervisor, the CEO, or anyone else, and eventually, unsure about their future with the organization, they decide to move on.

Like a true scientist, Kotch takes a survival of the fittest approach to employee development. "I believe in natural selection," he says. "I think one of my jobs as a manager is to create an environment where those employees who are talented and want to be developed can move up, and the low performers who don't want to improve themselves eventually move out."

Manage Every Employee Differently

"Motivation is the art of getting people to do what you want them to do because they want to do it."

- Dwight D. Eisenhower

It's 9 p.m. on a Sunday evening and Angela Lewton is headed to work. Lewton, the director of marketing for a large computer company, doesn't work the night shift. Instead, she is going in for a few hours to "hang out" with one of her most talented employees. You see, Lewton has an exceptionally gifted brand manager we'll call "Jessica," who does her very best work late at night.

"Jessica is pretty much nocturnal," says Lewton. "But she's one of the most talented marketing people I've ever worked with, so if she wants to work late at night or early in the morning, that's fine with me. I'll do whatever I can to support her."

Unlike some managers who espouse "treating all employees the same," Lewton gets it. She understands that all employees are a little bit different and need to be coached and motivated in different ways. Over the years, Lewton has made a variety of accommodations for high performing employees, including allowing for flexible schedules, telecommuting, and putting together "creative" compensation packages. Lewton also gives some employees a great deal of feedback while practically leaving others alone depending on which leadership style results in the best performance. "Obviously, I'm not a believer in a one-style-fits-all approach to management," says Lewton.

In Jessica's case, Lewton insists she does not "favor" her talented employee, but she is quite open about the fact that she "accommodates" her. "At the end of the day, my job as a manager is to get the best per-formance out of employees who work for me," she says. "If I can help raise her performance by showing some flexibility, by all means, that's what I'm going to do."

"I'm not a believer in a one-style-fits-all approach to management."

Angela Lewton, High Tech Executive

One of the accommoda-tions Lewton makes for Jessica is trying not to schedule meetings for her before 11:00 a.m. Some managers would be appalled by such an action, but Lewton is undeterred. "I think one of the rea-sons I've been able to retain Jessica is that I'm flexible with her schedule and I allow her a lot of creative freedom," says Lewton.

Lewton knows there is a downside to her unconven-tional approach. She understands that once you "open the door" and start offering flexibility to one individual, other employees will want similar treatment. "I tell all of my em-ployees from day one that any type of special schedule, vari-able compensation, or anything out of the ordinary is earned based on performance over time," she says.

Jessica has worked for Lewton for more than seven years and during that time Jessica has received numerous job offers including one from sports television powerhouse ESPN. "The ESPN people wanted her badly and offered about five times what I could pay her," says Lewton. "Frankly, I told her it was too good an opportunity to pass up and she should take the job."

But in the end, Jessica turned down the big bucks and decided she wanted to stay and continue working with Lewton. "I don't think I did anything special to keep her. I just tried to be a little flexible and manage her a little differently than some of my other employees," says Lewton. "I can pretty much guarantee that if I had been insisting she work 9:00 am to 5:00 pm, I would have lost her long ago."

Get in the Trenches Once in a While

"Delegating work works, provided the one delegating works, too."

- Robert Half

It is pouring rain and the winds are howling on a fall day in Eagle, Idaho. Customers at WinCo Foods, one of the Northwest's fastest growing grocery chains, are dashing in and out of the store trying to escape the nasty weather. However, two employees stay out in the downpour, gathering wayward shopping carts. One worker is a teenage cart boy, pretty much the low man on the totem pole in the grocery store hierarchy. The other employee getting soaked is Linda Chandler, the store manager and a WinCo veteran of 26 years.

Chandler could certainly dispatch one of her 150-plus employees to perform cart duty, but that's not her style. "I've always thought a leader should be willing to do any job the employees do," says Chandler. "When I was an employee, the managers I admired most were the ones who would jump in and work during difficult times in the store."

Chandler has also cleaned flooded bathrooms, shoveled snow from in front of the store, and mopped up dozens of spills during her 13 years as a manager. "The uglier the job, the better," she says. "If there is a major problem in the bathroom, I'll take the job. It gives me a chance to show the employees I'm not above doing whatever they are asked to do."

While Chandler preaches the importance of "leading by example," she stresses that a good manager also needs to be careful not to jump into every crisis. "One thing I see with a lot of young managers is that they spend all of their time on the floor reacting to every little crisis," says Chandler. "One minute they're in the check stand, the next moment they're moving freight, and then they're fixing all the displays. Basically the store manager is acting like an employee and that's not what they're being paid to do."

"I've always thought a leader should be willing to do any job the employees do."

Linda Chandler, Store Manager
WinCo Foods

Chandler believes good managers spend most of their time focusing on "big picture" issues like strategy, operations, and training. However, she stresses the importance of "picking your spots" and knowing when it is time to jump in and work side-by-side with employees. "Obviously, I spend most of my time running the day-to-day operations of the store because that's what I'm ultimately evaluated on," she says. "I need to resist the temptation to try and solve every problem. In most cases, my time is better spent training or delegating to other employees so they can develop the skills to solve problems in the future."

Chandler does not think there's a magic number in terms of what percentage of her time should be spent "in the trenches working with employees." Instead, she relies on her experience and intuition to decide when it's time to roll up her sleeves and get into the fray. "Generally, I dig in and work when things are most stressful and chaotic," she says. "That's when employees may be getting down or frustrated and that's when they need to see that the leader of the store is working right there beside them."

Simple Strategy #5

Stay Cool When Things Heat Up

"The only safe ship in a storm is leadership."

- Faye Wattleton

So you think you've got pressure at work? Consider Dr. Renee Bobrowski, a perinatologist, who is leading a 10-person medical team as they perform an emergency caesarean section on a high risk mother and her baby. In this instance, Bobrowski is delivering a little girl in distress, whose blood pressure is dropping rapidly. Dr. Bobrowski has done hundreds of these deliveries and knows she has approximately 10 to 15 minutes to deliver the child or the consequences will be dire.

You might think the operating room would be chaos, but it is actually eerily calm. Bobrowski chats with her team in a composed, reassuring voice and they respond in a professional manner. No one barks out orders, races around the room, or panics. "The last thing I'm going to do in a crisis situation is start yelling orders and throwing instruments around the room," says Bobrowski. "I saw doctors do that when I was training and it was ridiculous. The nurses were so nervous their hands were shaking."

Instead, Bobrowski makes a conscious effort to slow things down during a crisis situation. "I try to speak very clearly and precisely when things are tense," she says. "If I need someone's attention, I call them by their first name, but

I don't yell or raise my voice. It's my job to keep people calm, not stress them out."

Business leaders could learn a lot from Bobrowski's calm, reasoned style of leadership during a period of crisis.

I've found that extreme stress often results in poor leadership behavior. During times of crisis, I've all too often seen leaders:

- **Lose control.** It amazes me that high level executives still throw temper tantrums, but it happens every day. College educated men and women in thousand dollar suits acting like four-year-olds, stomping around the board room when something goes wrong. Executives often behave this way because threats and anger actually work as short-term motivators. However, in the long run, leaders who frequently become unhinged get very little respect and almost no loyalty from their employees.

> *"The last thing I'm going to do in a crisis situation is start yelling orders and throwing instruments around the room."*
>
> Renee Bobrowski, M.D.
> Saint Alphonsus
> Medical Group

- **Huddle behind closed doors.** During tough financial times, executives tend to do a lot of huddling behind closed doors. Unfortunately, these secret meetings usually result in full-scale paranoia among the employees, who spend most of their time speculating about who will be the first to get the axe. Company leaders should be more visible than ever during periods of crisis. In addition, executives should share as much information as possible with employees, as long as they don't make promises they can't keep.

- **Lose perspective.** The best leaders I know are able to keep problems in perspective. They don't reorganize the company when the sales numbers dip for a quarter and they don't lose their screws and start firing people when operational mistakes are made. Instead, strong leaders keep an eye on the big picture. They gather as much data as possible and also rely on past experiences and historical perspective when navigating the rough waters of corporate America.

Mishandling a crisis can devastate an organization. When leaders blow their tops or lose perspective and over-react, the most common results are poor morale, a drop in employee production, and increased turnover (see Simple Strategy 10).

Bobrowski uses a boating metaphor to emphasize the importance of remaining calm in a crisis: "When you're in charge of an operating room you're like a captain commanding a boat," she says. "If I freak out and start yelling at people, the crew is going to fall apart and eventually the boat is going to run aground."

Take Care of Your Stars

"Great ability reveals itself increasingly with each new assignment."

- Baltasar Gracian

Forget the politically correct bull you've heard in your management training classes about "treating all employees equally." Stop wasting your time with that bottom 20% of your workforce. I am here to tell you that the smartest leaders take care of their superstars and they're proud of it.

Do you think sports superstars Kobe Bryant or Alex Rodriguez are treated the same way as their less talented teammates by their coaches and team owners? No way. You can play with mediocre talent, but to win championships, or to achieve great success in the corporate world, you need superstars.

A survey conducted by the Gallup Organization found that the typical American company has a high percentage of average to above average performers (about 70%), a certain number of low performers (about 20%), and a small percentage of superstars (usually 10% or less). Common sense tells us that the quickest way to bankruptcy is to lose your top performers. However, research tells us that most corporations sink countless hours and millions of dollars into trying to salvage their low performers as opposed to investing time and dollars into their stars.

As a small business owner myself, I practice a simple philosophy. I put my best person on my biggest opportunity. While I strive to treat all of my employees consistently (which is different than equally) and respectfully, if I have extra time or financial resources, I devote them to support my top performers. Don't get me wrong. I certainly appreciate the hard work and dedication of my "scrappy," overachieving solid performers, but it is the superstars who are paying the rent and keeping the electricity on.

Common sense tells us that the quickest way to bankruptcy is to lose your top performers.

So, how do you make certain your competitors don't swipe your big guns away? A few suggestions:

- **Acknowledge your stars.** Step number one is incredibly simple and won't cost you a nickel. Begin by telling your star employees how much you appreciate them and that they have a bright future with your organization. I cannot tell you how many times one of my clients has lost a top employee, and during their exit interview, the employee states that, "I didn't really feel appreciated," or "I didn't know if I had a future here."

- **Talk about the future.** Most high achieving employees are hungry to move up. Make sure they know opportunities exist in your company or they may seek greener pastures elsewhere. Sit down with your superstars and discuss possible career paths within your organization. You should also ask them what they'd like to do in the future. Don't assume you know their desired career path because you may be wrong.

- **Pay up, right now.** Another simple strategy for retaining top performers is to pay people what they are worth, when they are worth it (see Simple Strategy 22). If you have a saleswoman who is closing deals like crazy, walk into her office today and give her a raise. Don't be shortsighted and squeeze a few months out of her on the cheap. And don't wait until her next performance review to boost her pay. The competition may have hired her by then.

- **Make life interesting.** Feeling challenged is just as important to high performers as being well compensated. Star employees constantly want to be acquiring new skills. You never want your top people to get bored or they may decide to look for something more interesting to do.

There are very few truly exceptional performers in the workforce. If you and your organization are going to thrive, it is essential to identify your exceptional people and take proactive steps to hang on to them. Because if you don't take care of your superstars, the competition will.

Part II

SIMPLE
COMMUNICATION
STRATEGIES

Communicate with Your Feet

"The greatest problem in communication is the illusion it has taken place."

- George Bernard Shaw

Large law firms can be brutal places to work. The office politics are vicious, the infighting relentless, and the rumor mill works overtime. Think about how the typical large firm operates. First, you hire dozens of highly intelligent, ambitious young attorneys. Then, you put them in an ultra-competitive environment where success is judged by criteria like hundreds of hours billed, business brought to the firm, and who sucks up most to the senior partners. Talk about a recipe for disaster. What most firms wind up with is high turnover and a bunch of stressed out attorneys and staff members who hate their jobs.

However, a law firm based in Pittsburgh, Pennsylvania, has avoided that type of toxic work environment. In fact, employees with Reed Smith, which employs 1,300 attorneys worldwide, are pretty happy. And much of the credit should go to their managing partner, Greg Jordan. Since Jordan began running Reed Smith in 2000, the firm has enjoyed incredible financial success (tripling revenues in six years) while maintaining strong employee morale. "What I'm most proud of is that during this time of growth, we haven't had a single equity partner leave our organization," says Jordan. "We work hard to make this an enjoyable place to work and people tend to stay."

LEADERSHIP ISN'T ROCKET SCIENCE

So what exactly does Jordan do to help create such a positive environment?

"I spend a lot of my time walking around talking to people," he says. "I talk to the partners, I talk to the employees, and I talk to the new recruits. I basically talk to anyone who will talk to me. I believe that communicating with employees and knowing what they're thinking and feeling is perhaps the most important aspect of my job."

> **"I spend a lot of my time walking around talking to people."**
>
> Greg Jordan, Managing Partner
> Reed Smith Law Firm

In some ways, Jordan acts as Reed Smith's chief morale officer. Jordan, an outgoing, likable executive who's usually flashing a big smile, is the kind of guy who, in 10 minutes, can make you feel like you've known him your entire life. "Law firms have always been known as dark and secretive. People envision a black box being passed around by the partners in a smoky boardroom," says Jordan. "We try to turn that upside down and focus on creating a more open, enjoyable environment."

Research on employee morale consistently shows that "poor communication" by company leaders is a primary reason for low morale and high turnover. Jordan is keenly aware of these facts and, if anything, he is determined to almost over-communicate with employees. In addition to this "managing with his feet" approach to leadership, Jordan utilizes some other simple strategies for effectively communicating with employees:

- **Push away from email and hit the road.** "I probably spend at least half my time traveling so that I can meet face-to-face with employees. We have new offices in France, England, and Germany, and there's too much lost in my message if I try to communicate with these employees via email. I need to sit across from people to understand their questions and concerns."

- **Ask dozens of questions.** "When I sit down with employees I try to do less talking and more asking questions and listening. If there is a problem, I want to try and be in front of it instead of reacting to it. The only way to know employee concerns is to ask lots of questions."

- **Show employees the important stuff.** "We absolutely open up the books to the employees, which some law firms consider taboo. We communicate our financials so that they have an understanding of the health of the firm," says Jordan. "These are smart people and if you want them to buy in, you need to give them facts and tell them how things are going. Basically, we try to communicate just about everything."

Let Go of the Lingo

"Our business is infested with idiots who try to impress by using

pretentious jargon."

- David Ogilvy

Jack, a marketing executive with a multi-million dollar high-tech organization, strolls five minutes late into his weekly department meeting. He sits down, eyes his staff, and, I kid you not, says: "I'm concerned about our human capital. I'm not sure we possess the head count or the bandwidth to achieve these deliverables." Jack's staff looks at him in stunned silence, not knowing how to respond.

Barely taking a breath, Jack continues his jargon-filled monologue, encouraging his team to get out of their "silos," "follow their critical path," and "create synergies" in order to become a "world class organization." Jack also manages to review the marketing strategy from "30,000 feet" and he even touches on the organization's "value proposition."

I don't think anyone in the room knew exactly what Jack was talking about. I'm not even sure Jack knew what he was saying. One thing was certain, however: his message was not well received. Employees rolled their eyes, shook their heads, or stared at Jack in disbelief. Everything about their nonverbal communication said, "This guy can't be serious."

Although these buzzwords and phrases are catchy and clever, they are also overused, condescending, and often so vague they can't be interpreted. Jack spoke a lot, without really saying anything at all. When I spoke to Jack later that day, I gave him some simple advice. I told him to scrap the business school vocabulary and start talking to his employees like real people. I encouraged Jack to use common, everyday language, to be more specific in his directions, and to do more listening and less talking.

In contrast to Jack, meet Matt McCormick, director of sales for Peet's Coffee in Emeryville, California. McCormick, the consummate high energy, affable salesman, begins to laugh when asked about the pervasive use of business jargon in the corpo-

> **"How are the sales-people supposed to achieve their goals if they don't understand them?"**
>
> Matt McCormick, Director of Sales
> Peet's Coffee

rate world. "As the person in charge of sales for the organization, it's my job to help employees understand the company strategy, not cause further confusion," he says. "How are the salespeople supposed to achieve their goals if they don't understand them?"

You will not hear McCormick telling a member of his sales force they need to have a "side bar." Instead, he will have a discussion. And he won't "deep six" a project. He will get rid of it. "Sometimes business executives get pretty full of themselves," he says. "When they're spouting a bunch of lingo, they're actually doing more harm than good."

McCormick is known at Peet's for his straightforward but respectful style. He holds personal meetings with each of his salespeople each week to specifically discuss team goals and individual performance. "I think I surprise employees sometimes with my honesty," he says. "Some of them think I'm a little crazy because they're not used to direct communication in the corporate world. In the business world, people are used to communication being indirect, bureaucratic, and confusing."

A simple communication strategy McCormick utilizes is to regularly write out and distribute the sales department's Top Five Goals. The goals are deliberately written in a simple, concise manner. You will not find one of McCormick's goals focused on "achieving incremental growth by capitalizing on innovative sales channels." Instead one of this year's goals is to "Hit the number 75." The 75 in this case refers to 75 million dollars in total sales. "There's plenty of time to get into the details about how we're going to achieve things, but it all starts with communicating the overall strategy."

McCormick adds, "My job is to give employees the best possible chance to succeed and they aren't ever going to be successful if they don't have a clear understanding of what you want from them."

Stop Talking and Start Listening

"When people talk, listen completely. Most people never listen."

- Ernest Hemingway

Humans are terrible listeners. Most of us love to talk, but we are dreadful when it comes to listening. Consider these statistics:

- The average employee retains less than 10% of what he or she hears in a meeting just two hours after its completion.

- When introduced to a stranger, more than half of us have forgotten that individual's name just seconds after being introduced.

Working with a management team recently, I looked around the room and noticed something very interesting, and more than a little frightening. Six of the seven individuals sitting around the power conference table were speaking at the same time and none of them was listening to a word others were saying. Not surprisingly, the person sitting quietly attempting to decipher the chaos was the one woman on the management team.

Research tells us that women are better listeners than men. Women aren't great listeners, just a lot better than men. When it comes to listening, men are basically a lost cause.

Some researchers believe women are simply born better listeners. Others feel that environmental factors, such as being the primary caretakers of children, have resulted in women having superior listening skills. I tend to vote for the environmental influences. It's not unusual to see girls as young as four or five sitting across from one another listening and really communicating. The little girls nod their heads and give their full, undivided attention. Some males go their entire lives without having this type of conversation. In fact, when possible, men prefer to speak to one another sitting side-by-side on bar stools or at an athletic event.

When it comes to listening, men are basically a lost cause.

If you're unsure about your own listening skills, take the following true/false quiz:

1. I often find myself finishing other people's sentences.

2. I often daydream when my work colleagues are speaking.

3. I sometimes take phone calls or check my email when I am in the middle of a face-to-face discussion with a co-worker.

4. How closely I listen varies a great deal depending upon who is speaking.

5. I often fake like I am listening to a speaker when I am really not.

If you answered "true" to three or more of the above statements, you are likely among the acoustically challenged and probably won't ever be a great listener. However, you can use a few simple strategies to improve your skills. Here are three of my favorites:

- **Limit distractions.** Get off your cell phone, push away from your laptop, turn off your pager, and give your colleague your full attention. Temporarily breaking away from your high-tech business toys will improve your chances of retaining what is being said. Simultaneously it sends a powerful non-verbal message to your peer that what he or she is saying is important. And if you really want to blow your colleague away, consider taking out a note pad and writing down the highlights of what is being said.

- **Stop finishing the speaker's sentences.** If you suspect you are guilty of this common listening problem, spend one day saying "I apologize" or "excuse me" each time you respond before the speaker completes his or her sentence. My guess is you will get into double digits pretty fast. One way to overcome this annoying habit is to wait for the speaker to finish and then say "1001" in your head before responding.

- **Paraphrase.** I am not suggesting you give a corny therapeutic response such as, "What I hear you saying is..." each time one of your colleagues finishes a sentence. However, briefly attempting to recap what an individual has just said is a wonderful way to make certain you have the gist of the message.

Just to recap, most people, especially us guys, are dreadful listeners. However, you can dramatically improve your odds of retaining what is being communicated by employing specific listening strategies.

Erupt at Your Own Risk

"You don't lead by hitting people over the head—that's assault,

not leadership."

- Dwight D. Eisenhower

Sarah, a sales executive, could see the explosion coming. She had heard the rumors about her manager's infamous temper, but this was the first time she would witness it first-hand. "I was a high performing employee, so in my first two years in the company, I hadn't seen him explode," says Sarah. "But I made a major mistake with a key account and I knew the volcano was about to erupt."

And erupt it did. Sarah's boss stomped around his office, raising his voice and using the "F-word" as a noun, a verb, and an adjective. "He lost it," says Sarah. "I didn't think that would happen in a professional environment, but the guy came completely unhinged."

Sarah's experience is not unusual. I have seen well-educated, highly paid executives lose their screws many times. One minute they are looking cool and composed while dealing with clients or the board of directors, and the next thing you know, they are raging through the hallways throwing a tantrum that would make a first grader proud.

Typically, executives rationalize their behavior with clichés like "I'm just using tough love," or "If you can't take the heat, you should get out." More often than not, employees do just that. In Sarah's case, she was gone in six months.

"I was at a point in my career where I wasn't going to let anybody treat me like that."

I am a strong believer that one public "meltdown" by a manager is all it takes to lose the respect of your employees. And if a supervisor is verbally abusing employees in public, look out. It is just a matter of time until good employees start parading out the front door of your organization.

"I believe the minute you blow up at an employee, you've lost their respect," says Tabb Compton, sales manager for Crucial Technology. "They may not leave that day, but they will eventually. And if they don't leave, they'll make you pay somehow by destroying a project or just by not giving you their best effort."

> **"I believe the minute you blow up at an employee, you've lost their respect."**
>
> **Tabb Compton, Sales Manager**
> **Crucial Technology**

Compton, who previously owned a small business and worked as head of operations for a benefits company, is known for his calm, rational approach toward employee management. In 20-plus years in corporate leadership, he says he can't ever remember yelling at or belittling an employee. "What would I accomplish by doing that," he asks. "My job as a leader is to portray stability and consistency. How can I expect employees to perform at a high level when they don't know whether you're going to blow up at any moment?"

You won't find Compton going ballistic regardless of the mistakes his employees make. Instead, he takes a more understated and humble approach. "Obviously, I address the employee privately," he says. "I don't sugar-coat things, but I never raise my voice or put them down. In most cases, I also take some of the responsibility for the error, because it's quite possible I didn't train them or prepare them properly."

Don't get me wrong. I'm not suggesting managers shy away from holding employees accountable. Good managers set high standards and discipline employees when those standards aren't met. But there is a big difference between being strict and being abusive. If employees wanted to have profanity screamed in their faces, they would have joined the Marine Corps, not corporate America.

Don't Manage by Email

"Face-to-face communication remains the most powerful interaction."

- Kathleen Begley

Charles, the president of a small software company, couldn't seem to push away from his computer. As the top executive in the organization, he received as many as 200 emails a day and he was bound and determined to respond to each one. "It is how I like to communicate," Charles told me after I was hired by the company's board of directors to help him improve his communication skills. "Email is efficient and concise. I can practically run the company from my computer terminal."

No question about it, email is an excellent business tool. However, the only place Charles was running the company with his "management by email" approach was into the ground. What Charles failed to realize is that email is fine for scheduling appointments and relaying simple information, but electronic communication is not a good tool for coaching employees, resolving conflict, or communicating anything that might be misinterpreted.

Charles eventually learned that many of his concise emails were being misunderstood. "People were confusing my messages," he said. "People were thinking I was ticked off at them because my messages were short and to the point."

Something to keep in mind is that a great deal of communication is nonverbal (some studies say as much as 80-90%). And obviously, the receiver of an email cannot see your nonverbal behavior. So, unless you can paint a word picture like Mark Twain or John Steinbeck, I suggest you get on the phone, or better yet, meet face-to-face with colleagues when relaying sensitive information. According to a study in the Journal of Personality and Social Psychology, there is a 50% chance each email you send will be misinterpreted.

There is a 50% chance each email you send will be misinterpreted.
Journal of Personality and Social Psychology

I have seen quite a few managers get into hot water when they utilize email inappropriately. Here are some simple suggestions for utilizing email effectively:

- **Never send an emotionally charged email.** If you are angry about a "nasty-gram" you have just received from a colleague, don't jump into the gutter with them and respond in kind. Instead, pick up the phone or walk down the hall to resolve the problem.

- **Never reprimand someone via email.** Have enough backbone to meet face-to-face with someone when disciplining them.

- **Start a new message with a greeting (i.e. "Hi, Jack").** If you simply launch into what you need from the individual without some type of hello, you will likely be perceived as pushy.

- **Do not copy someone's boss on an email unless there is a legitimate business reason.** One of the most common tactics I see these days is for employees to show one another up by copying critical emails to the boss. This tactic is unkind, unwise, and apt to boomerang on you.

- **Assume the worst.** If you've re-written an email five times because you're afraid it may be misinterpreted, do not hit the "send" button. I can assure you, confusing or emotional emails will be misunderstood just about every time. My suggestion is to get on the phone or walk down the hall and talk to your co-worker face-to-face.

Despite these potential email pitfalls, I'm not suggesting for a minute that you eliminate or even limit email usage. I would, however, suggest you proceed with caution. Poorly written email correspondence can result in a great deal of confusion and resentment. Even in the age of the laptop and the Blackberry, sometimes it's still best to communicate face-to-face.

Assess and Assist Troubled Employees

"The key to leadership today is influence, not authority."

- Ken Blanchard

I will never forget the first executive coaching project I had with a physician. I received a call from an administrator at a large hospital in the Northwest about a surgeon who had "an anger management problem." Unfortunately, this doctor's temper had recently gotten the best of him and he had hurled a clipboard across an exam room and hit a defenseless nurse. After further inquiry, I learned that this was not Dr. Happy's first temper tantrum. He had a long history of creating a hostile environment for colleagues with abusive language, demeaning comments, and aggressive behavior.

Since that first call, I have coached more than 100 physicians and most of them were far less belligerent than my first client. However, I can assure you not a lot of interpersonal skills are taught in American medical schools and doctors generally do not make the most caring and supportive co-workers. Most physicians are highly intelligent, strongly opinionated, and often possess good-sized egos. It is what makes them good doctors, but sometimes bad team members.

"Many doctors struggle with teamwork. It's not something that's emphasized in our training," says Dr. Michael Roach, medical director for St. Alphonsus Medical Group in Boise, Idaho. "Doctors can be abrupt and overly concerned about maintaining their authority over the staff."

Roach has been managing physicians for years and is currently responsible for about 100 doctors. So how would he handle our projectile-throwing physician? "With really outrageous behavior, I start from the perspective that we probably aren't going to cure the problem. When someone is this out of control, the best we can probably do is manage the person and try to minimize the behavior. Then

> *"My experience with doctors is that some of them don't even realize the destructive impact they're having on their staffs."*
>
> **Michael Roach, Medical Director**
> **Saint Alphonsus Medical Group**

the organization has to decide if this individual is worth the risk."

Roach believes, and I strongly agree with him, that "some personalities are just too problematic," and in those instances, the organization needs to "part ways" with the physician (see Simple Strategy 25). However, Roach believes most behavior problems can be significantly improved. Roach addresses physician interpersonal issues much like he does medical problems. He begins by gathering information and then starts to formulate a plan. "I never rush into a situation and confront the doctor. Instead, I try to ask a lot of questions and understand the physician's perspective. Then I work with the doctor to come up with solutions. I also always schedule some type of follow-up."

Roach is basically suggesting a three-step process to address physician behavior problems and I would argue his approach is relevant to any group of employees.

1. Diagnose the problem by asking lots of questions.

2. Design and implement a treatment plan to correct problem behaviors.

3. Follow-up to assess how the individual is progressing.

I don't care if you're managing doctors, lawyers, engineers, or electricians, Roach's simple approach to correcting problem behavior is a good one. In order to change bad behavior, employees must first understand what they're doing wrong. Next, they need suggestions for better, more productive actions they can take. Finally, it is essential that their new behavior is measured or at least monitored to track progress.

"My experience with doctors is that some of them don't even realize the destructive impact they're having on their staffs," says Roach. "If you just listen to them, educate them and support the changes you've asked them to make, you can often be successful in improving behavior."

Assert Yourself

"The only healthy style of communication is assertive communication."

- John Rohn

I once witnessed a communication blunder of epic proportions perpetrated by the CEO of a small retail organization. The company's peak season was quickly approaching and he decided to send out an email that went something like the following: "Our busy season is coming up and everyone must give it 100% for us to be successful. Last year, some of you performed well, but some of you didn't pull your weight. You know who you are."

As you might expect, this communication masterpiece did not go over well with the workforce. Basically, all 100-plus employees stopped working and started gossiping in an effort to figure out who the boss was talking about. As a result, production plummeted, creating the exact opposite reaction he had hoped for. I would also hazard a guess that the "low performing employees" were clueless that he was talking about them while some of his high performers were terrified that their jobs were at risk.

When I asked the CEO a few weeks later how many low performers he was talking about in his email message he said, "About six or seven." He went on to say, "Actually, I'm very happy with about 90% of the workforce." Unfortunately, in an effort to deliver a message to a half dozen slackers, he alienated a good portion of his workforce.

So here's the key question: Why did this CEO send out a company-wide email instead of confronting these six or seven employees directly?

Passive managers tend to water down their messages, but you owe it to your employees to give it to them straight.

"I don't like conflict," he says. "I didn't want to deal with employees crying or getting defensive with me. I just wanted them to do their jobs."

Explanations like his are common among passive leaders who are highly resistant to what they perceive as conflict. Often they are very nice people, but their conflict phobia can create a great deal of confusion and enormous cost to their organizations, because they are slow in confronting problems and hesitate to communicate directly and clearly.

When working with passive, indirect leaders my message is very simple: Assert yourself. It is not easy for those who are introverted, conflict-avoidant leaders. Most of them would rather have a root canal than confront a tough issue in a timely manner. But in some instances, there is simply no other choice. For those of you who dread these types of discussions, here are a few suggestions:

- **Be direct.** Passive managers tend to water down their messages, but you owe it to your employees to give it to them straight. Don't say, "I need you to do a little better, if that's possible." Say, "I need you to increase production so that you're meeting standard for the company."

- **Be specific.** Indirect leaders often fail to provide specifics when communicating with struggling employees. They also tend to rely on business clichés that make them feel good, but leave employees wondering what you are talking about. Don't say, "I need you to give me 110%." Say, "You're currently billing 20 invoices a day and the rest of the team averages 30. What can we do to improve your performance?"

- **Do not be aggressive.** Many managers think they are being assertive when they are actually being aggressive. A statement like, "You better hit those numbers or else," is direct, but it is an ultimatum. Try saying, "It's crucial that we hit those numbers, what do we need to do to make it happen?" Make certain your communication is direct, but also respectful.

- **Don't be sarcastic.** Sarcasm is an indirect and facetious style of communication that often frustrates and angers co-workers. Don't say, "Hey, Einstein, isn't that project done yet?" Say, "It's crucial that we get that project done today. What can I do to help?"

I can't guarantee you that utilizing assertive communication will result in success, but it does give you the best opportunity to deliver a clear message. In particular, when providing employees input on performance, the best communicators are direct, specific, and respectful.

Part III

SIMPLE
BUSINESS
STRATEGIES

Simplify Systems and Strategy

"So much of what we call management consists in making it difficult for

people to work."

- Peter Drucker

The average middle manager in America spends about 12 hours per week in meetings. The typical company handbook is 45 pages long. These are the types of statistics that make Bill Long, the former CEO and now chairman of WinCo Foods, shake his head. "If company executives would just get out of the way of their employees, maybe more organizations would be successful," says Long.

WinCo, an employee-owned company, is a rare example of a company that truly practices a "less is more" philosophy. "All of our company policies are written on one legal size piece of paper," says Long. "We want our people focused on selling groceries, not on dozens of different rules and regulations."

As for meetings, you won't see many of those at WinCo either. Store managers are encouraged, but not required, to have an hour-long meeting once a week. First-line supervisors are asked to hold one meeting a quarter. WinCo's company executives don't feel a large number of meetings are necessary because, like everything else at WinCo, the organization's business model is ultra simple. "We haven't really changed our philosophy since day one in 1978," says Long. "We offer lower prices than anybody in the business and we do whatever we can to cut our expenses so that we're able to offer those low prices. It's pretty much that simple."

WinCo does not accept credit cards and customers have to bag their own groceries. Some might say the company is "out of touch," but in reality, the strategy is genius in its simplicity. WinCo is highly profitable, rapidly growing, and one of the few retailers in the country that successfully competes head-to-head with Wal-Mart.

> **"If company executives would just get out of the way of their employees, maybe more organizations would be successful."**
> Bill Long, Chairman of the Board
> WinCo Foods

Over the years, I have seen many companies experiencing periods of great success build palatial corporate headquarters as monuments to mark their success. Not WinCo. Instead, the company just added on to their current headquarters, a modest building on the outskirts of Boise, Idaho. In fact, WinCo's headquarters looks a lot like one of the company's stores. It is functional and clean, but extremely understated for a company doing nearly five billion dollars a year in sales.

You won't find a bunch of vice presidents roaming the halls at WinCo either. The organization employees about half as many VPs as most retail organizations of its size. "We're an employee-owned company so we work very hard to stay lean," says Long, who was known to occasionally throw freight or jump into a check stand when the need would arise. "If we have a bunch of unnecessary executive positions, that's money out of the employees' pockets."

Long acknowledges that over the years there has been outside pressure to change the way WinCo does business. Consultants and industry experts have recommended trendier, flashier marketing and displays for WinCo's stores. "I can remember board meetings when we discussed the pros and cons of things like coffee bars...but in the end, that didn't fit us...we've always decided to stay focused on being the low cost leader in the industry. It may not be real exciting to some, but it's what we do best."

Make Your Mission Meaningful

"Life is really simple, but we insist on making it complicated."

- Confucius

The mission statement of a typical large American company goes something like this: "To be the most effective, strategic, and customer-focused company in the industry with exceptional processes and operations that annually provide significant returns to its shareholders." The same company usually has between seven and 10 values including "integrity," "humility," and "innovation." And if the employees are really lucky, the organization might even have a vision statement, a strategic purpose, and possibly even a company motto.

The organization's mission and values are usually created by company executives during a retreat to some exotic location like Maui or Aspen. Apparently, company bigwigs are more creative when retreating at five-star resorts. Hours are spent crafting just the right language, every word discussed and debated at length. All too often, when the management team returns from the mountaintop and rolls out its words of wisdom, most employees could care less. To them, it's all just business speak by a bunch of high-paid people with an inflated sense of themselves.

In fact, when I go into companies and start asking employees about their organization's mission statement, fewer than 5% can recite even a couple of words. Even rarer is the employee who can come up with the company values, vision statement, etc. That's because employees have been bombarded with so many strategies, missions, goals, and purposes that everything has washed together and become meaningless.

> "It's vital for management to make an organization's mission and vision understandable at the employee level."
>
> Faye Wattleton,
> Executive Director
> Center for Advancement
> of Women

"It's vital for management to make an organization's mission and vision understandable at the employee level," says Faye Wattleton, executive director for the Center for Advancement of Women. "Employees have to understand how their day-to-day duties relate to the goals of the organization."

Wattleton, who has also served on numerous corporate boards, believes executive teams often send their employees confusing or mixed messages because they are constantly changing their own minds about the direction of the organization. "Good organizations find out what they do well and then they execute it over and over again," she says. "These days, executives have no patience. If the company has a bad year or even a bad quarter, they restructure the company and change the strategy. American companies tend to throw the baby out with the bath water."

I agree with Wattleton. Patience and simplicity are rare virtues in corporate America these days. Company leaders are constantly confusing their employees with their ever-changing business strategies and inability to present a simple, understandable message.

One example of a company that has consistently preached a simple, understandable philosophy is Nordstrom's, the Seattle-based clothing retailer. From day one of employment, the organization communicates the core value "customer service above all else." It is simple, to the point, and tells Nordstrom's employees exactly what is expected of them.

The bottom line is that good companies and strong leaders are excellent at simplifying communication. There may be no better example than Abraham Lincoln, whose Gettysburg address is only two minutes in length. If Abe can summarize the importance of the Civil War in two minutes, you should be able to keep your strategic plan under 12 pages. I don't care how ingenious your strategy may be, it won't matter if your employees don't understand it. Here are a few suggestions for keeping messages clear and concise:

- **Cut it in half.** Take your company mission statement and goals and try to reduce them by half. Longer is not better. And when presenting important company information to employees avoid PowerPoint presentations with dozens of slides. I can assure you that you'll lose the audience after the first 10.

- **Use common language.** Do not try to wow the work force with your industry knowledge and your business school vocabulary. In particular, eliminate the use of business jargon and acronyms.

- **Hammer home the main points.** If you're lucky, your employees will retain two or three points from any one presentation or interaction. So decide on the main concepts you want employees to retain and hammer away at them over and over again.

Simple Strategy #16

Don't Wait for Reality to Mow You Down

"Reality bites and doesn't let go."

- Author unknown

J udy, the Vice President of Marketing for a telecommunications company, knew morale in her department was bad. Two of her directors were feuding and the department was basically split, with half backing one director and half backing the other. Judy, a likable, soften-spoken individual, tried to address the rift by preaching the importance of "teamwork" during weekly department meetings. She hoped her generalized, subtle message would result in the two senior employees "doing what was best for the marketing division."

Instead the office gossip and backbiting escalated and the unpleasant environment eventually resulted in decreased productivity, lapses in customer service, and even turnover of key personnel. "I hate conflict," said Judy. "I just wanted the whole problem to disappear and for these two employees to start acting like adults. But it never happened and my department really fell apart. I lost a couple of my best employees when they got fed up and left."

Judy made a common mistake that I have seen hundreds of managers make. She avoided the problem and hoped it would go away. Wrong. These types of problems don't disappear. In fact, if left unchecked, behavior and performance problems fester and get worse. Passive leaders, like Judy, dread assertively confronting aggressive employees. The truth is, Judy had no other choice and neither do you when confronting difficult employee and business situations.

Whether you are a first time supervisor or the CEO of a large corporation, a good leader has to tackle difficult issues as soon as they arise. Believe me, if the company is facing problems, the employees already know. In fact, they probably knew before you did.

> *"Believe me, reality always catches up and reality always wins."*
> Don Bailey, CEO
> Questcor Pharmaceuticals

My suggestion is to be brutally honest. If revenues are down, tell employees and ask for help in turning the situation around. If two supervisors are warring, get them in your office and get to the bottom of the problem. If you act like the ship is running smoothly when everyone knows it is sinking, you lose all credibility with employees.

"Denial is the downfall of a lot of leaders," says Don Bailey, CEO of Questcor Pharmaceuticals. "Many business leaders are entrepreneurs so they're eternal optimists. They often end up denying or avoiding problems in their organizations. But believe me, reality always catches up and reality always wins."

In his 25-plus years as a high tech and pharmaceutical executive, Bailey has faced about every business crisis you can imagine. He has dealt with product recalls, employee morale issues, media scrutiny, and worse. In fact, in his current position with Questcor, he was confronted with some harsh realities about two minutes after assuming his new leadership post. "It was obvious right away that our sales were flat and our cash flow situation wasn't very good," he says. "The previous leadership had been denying the problems, but they were staring us right in the face."

Bailey, an engineer by training, didn't get riled up about the challenges he discovered at Questcor. Instead he took a systematic approach to getting them solved. "I basically approach all business problems the same way," he says. "I gather all the facts as quickly as possible, get input from the relevant people, consider the options, and make the best choice for the company." Without delay and without denial.

Bailey's four-step process sounds logical to me. And it appears to be working because Questcor's earnings and stock price have more than doubled since he took over. So why don't more executives use his approach to crisis management?

"The worst decisions in business are made because executives let ego or emotions get involved in their decision-making process," he says. "They lose objectivity and deny the severity of the problems because they're emotionally invested. Reality eventually forces them to stop denying the problems, but by that time, it's often too late."

Take a Deep Breath
Before Reorganizing

"The more things change, the more they remain insane."

- Michael Fry

The mantra in corporate America these days seems to be "when in doubt, reorganize." Some corporations let one bad financial quarter dictate a major restructuring so Wall Street knows the company means business. Every day you read about another flailing corporate giant undergoing "a major reorganization."

In more cases than not, different doesn't mean better.

I've witnessed the following scenario dozens of times: A hot-shot new company executive is hired to help a sputtering organization and he immediately wants to put his "stamp" on things. He needs to justify his big salary so he "shakes things up" by reorganizing a couple of divisions or even the entire company. The first step is usually to have all employees re-interview for their jobs. Next, many employees get new titles, some get new offices or cubicles, and a few get canned. Voilà, the hot shot gets credit for making the "tough decisions that need to be made."

Don't get me wrong, if a company is struggling over a sustained period of time, then difficult strategic and personnel decisions must be made. But American companies have a tendency to go into "crisis mode" and manage from financial quarter to quarter instead of considering the long-term health of the organization. "Sometimes reorganizing makes the executives feel pretty good about themselves, but it doesn't do much for the health of the company," says John Sears, plant manager for Smoke Guard, a manufacturer of smoke containment systems. "It's also extremely traumatic for the employees."

Sears has yet to implement a significant reorganization in his 12-plus years at the helm of Smoke Guard's operations, instead choosing to "tweak things" based on economic conditions. However, he is quite familiar with the restructuring process, having been reorganized himself several times while working as an hourly employee and supervisor in several large manufacturing companies early in his career. "What I remember about all of them is that there would be lots of secret meetings and then we would get a new boss and some new responsibilities. Then about the time we were learning our new jobs, we would get another executive team and reorganize yet again."

> **"Sometimes reorganizing makes the executives feel pretty good about themselves, but it doesn't do much for the health of the company."**
>
> John Sears, Plant Manager
> Smoke Guard Smoke Systems

According to Sears, Smoke Guard, which has grown from a $500,000 business to more than 13 million dollars in sales in recent years, considered a major restructuring a few years back. "Many companies were doing vertical integration so I think our management team felt some pressure to do so as well. Ultimately, we decided not to and instead we stayed focused on our core business and our core products. I'm glad we didn't get swept up in making those changes because I think they would have killed us."

Sears certainly isn't opposed to restructuring if there is a business necessity, he just feels American executives are way too quick to play the "reorg" card. "If you need to make major changes to be competitive then obviously that's what has to be done," says Sears. "But I don't think executives consider the impact that restructuring has on the workforce. It's confusing to employees and can make them feel devalued, like some kind of commodity. I'm not against restructuring if it's warranted. It just shouldn't be the first option."

Develop Some Perspective

"Total absence of humor renders life impossible."

- Colette

A couple of years ago, I was hired by a marketing company to "mediate" a conflict between two women who were mid-level managers. As I began asking questions about the conflict, I quickly determined the firm needed a referee, not a consultant. It turns out the two had been involved in a long-running feud over "creative differences" on a project. Initially, they sniped at each other in meetings and gossiped about one another behind the scenes.

Tension between the two middle managers continued to build, and eventually, they had a heated argument and wound up engaged in a brief wrestling match in the middle of the company's break room. They had to be separated by their own employees.

Talk about leading by example.

While I have assisted dozens of organizations in resolving interpersonal conflicts over the years, this was one of only a handful I've seen escalate into a full-fledged physical confrontation. And it was the only time I had seen two women come to blows in the workplace. So I was curious to ask the company president how things got so bad. "They just lost all perspective and any sense of humor they might have had about themselves or the situation," he says. "We do marketing, not brain surgery. For goodness sake, learn to laugh at yourself once in a while."

I have always remembered the company president's comments about "losing all perspective and any sense of humor" because it is something I see every day. Corporate executives, lawyers, engineers, and other professionals get so wrapped up in power struggles and office politics that they end up behaving like petulant children in the school yard.

> *A little self-deprecating humor can go a long way toward showing employees that you are human.*

I later discovered that the problems with the two women wrestlers at the marketing company stemmed from having very different work styles. One was highly organized, structured, and insistent upon strict deadlines. The other was a conceptual, creative individual who was always making last minute changes. "Frankly, one of them was borderline obsessive compulsive and the other was a flaky creative-type," says the company president. "If they would have acknowledged some of their own quirks, and, God forbid, even joked about them, they might have made a really good team."

He's right. Employees enjoy working with colleagues and for leaders who have a good sense of humor and a healthy perspective about the workplace. On the other hand, they dread working for a self-absorbed manager who believes that closing the next sale or completing the next marketing project will determine the fate of mankind.

Come to think of it, most of the great leaders I have met or read about have at least occasionally made fun of themselves. A little self-deprecating humor can go a long way toward showing employees that you are human and every bit as capable of making mistakes as they are. Dwight D. Eisenhower, one of the few U. S. presidents known for having a little humility, put it well when he said, "A sense of humor is part of the art of leadership, of getting along with people, and of getting things done."

Part IV

SIMPLE
HUMAN
RESOURCE
STRATEGIES

Simple Strategy #19

Hire Well or Watch Out

"It's your people that make the ultimate difference."

- Frederick P. Brooks

When it comes to hiring employees, my advice is simple: Whenever possible, go with a proven commodity. When I'm planning to hire a new employee for my own company, the first candidates I consider are almost always people I've worked with in the past. I realize hiring a former colleague may not be as exciting as opening the position to the masses, but I know I'm getting someone with proven talent because I've seen the individual produce on a day-to-day basis.

Broadening your search to the newspaper and the Internet certainly gives you more options, but you'll also have to sift through dozens of job hoppers, loafers, and loons before you find a couple of decent candidates. And if you choose wrong, look out. You'll spend the next two years asking HR and Legal if you have enough written documentation to sack the nutcase who was supposed to be your next marketing superstar.

The problem with hiring unknown employees is that they lie. And some are very good at it. In fact, a variety of human resource studies in recent years have found that more than a third of what is written in a typical resume is embellished or an outright lie.

I understand there are times when you have no choice but to go with an unknown commodity. In those instances, I'm in favor of utilizing multiple strategies such as skill testing, personality profiles, and reference checks in order to get a true feel for a job candidate.

"It's amazing what people will say when you just let them talk."

Jennifer Miller, Director of Human Resources Electronic Controls Corporations

I'm also an advocate of using a little creativity in the interview process. Here are some of my interview suggestions along with thoughts from Jennifer Miller, director of human resources for Electronic Controls Company, who has interviewed hundreds (if not thousands) of applicants in her career:

- **Consider a tag-team approach.** Anyone can turn it on for 90 minutes with one interviewer, but when exposed to multiple people over an extended period of time, people eventually reveal their true selves. "Every candidate we consider meets at least six different people in the company," says Miller. "In addition, we bring them back at least three times, usually for a day of interviews, a lunch appointment, and a tour of the facility. We want candidates exposed to multiple people in different settings." Miller's approach may seem time consuming, but it's better to invest 10 or 12 hours up front than the hundreds of hours and thousands of dollars it will cost if you make a bad hire.

- **Let them talk.** Miller says she typically asks a concise, behavioral interview question and then gives the applicant the floor. "I just let them go," she says. "Some candidates are able to make a concise point, but others don't know when to stop talking or how to organize their thoughts. It's amazing what people will say when you just let them talk. Eventually you'll begin to get a true picture of the person."

- **Beware of business babble.** My radar goes up when I hear applicants talking about "paradigm shifts," "mission critical" projects, and "low-hanging fruit." Says Miller, "When I hear a lot of jargon, I usually suspect the candidate doesn't have much substance. I think people use those types of clichés because they don't have real life examples to share." I agree with Miller. My experience with job candidates who go heavy on the business jargon is that they present grand visions but deliver minimal results. My suggestion is to let them pick their "low-hanging fruit" with another company.

- **Check candidates out with the receptionist.** I can't tell you how many times I've seen a job candidate wow the executives, but treat the administrative staff like they're the little people. "That's one of the reasons we expose applicants to so many people," says Miller. "We want to make sure they're going to treat everyone with respect, not just the executives."

To recap, I'm a big fan of hiring former co-workers because you know you're getting proven talent. However, if that isn't an option, don't be afraid to get creative in the interview process. Put job applicants in different situations with different people and spend as much time as necessary up front so that you limit your chances of making a bad hire.

Simple Strategy #20

Hire Your Opposite

"If you surround yourself with yourself, that does not bring innovation."

- Craig Lardner

One of the most popular personality assessments used in the corporate world is the Myers-Briggs Type Indicator or MBTI. I often use it as a tool when working with management teams and I did so once with a group of leaders in the construction business. The results of the assessments showed 10 of the 12 members of the leadership team had virtually the same personality profile. Specifically, it was a personality type defined by characteristics such as exceptional work ethic, ultra-competitiveness, and a hard-charging nature.

The CEO was delighted by the outcome. He had achieved his goal of surrounding himself with a bunch of highly productive, "take-no-prisoners" clones. Basically, he hired 10 of himself. "We've got one of the toughest and hungriest management teams around," he said. "We're going to be unstoppable."

As it turns out, there was something unstoppable in the following year. Employee turnover. Because of all the alpha-male executives, the workforce was extremely productive for about three weeks. Then, the floodgates opened and employees started streaming out because the working environment was about as enjoyable as boot camp.

It's one thing to have two or three "Type-A" personalities on an executive team, but 10 or 12 of the same type is another story. It turned out to be a recipe for 200% turnover. This CEO learned a painful lesson as he watched dozens of talented people leave his organization. Too many of one personality type in an organization is never a good thing.

I've seen the same mistake made when an employee-friendly leader surrounds himself with a bunch of managers who are "warm and fuzzy." It's a really enjoyable place to work and everyone likes one another right up until the point where people start losing their jobs because the company isn't productive enough.

> **The bottom line is that too many of one personality type in an organization is never a good thing.**

If left to our own devices, most of us will hire people just like ourselves because that's what we're comfortable with. To counter this temptation to essentially hire yourself, it's crucial that you identify what traits and skills your organization is lacking. Then you can search for people who possess complementary skills.

If you're a "butt kicker," hire someone friendly and approachable. If you're highly analytical, hire a strong conceptual thinker. If you're disorganized, hire someone well organized. The best organizations employ a wide variety of personalities with a broad range of skills. In fact, in many instances, the best person to hire is someone who is your opposite.

Having a diverse group of personalities is especially important when it comes to leadership teams. Over the years, the strongest executive teams I've seen have been diverse. Strong teams need to engage in passionate debate in order to make the best decisions for their organizations. However, if there's no diversity in how the members of the team think, ideas will go unchallenged and different perspectives unheard.

Broaden Your Hiring Horizons

"There is no substitute for talent."

- Aldous Huxley

I don't believe in quotas and I'm not a big fan of affirmative action hiring. In my opinion, forcing companies to hire a certain number of people from specific demographic groups is not in the best interest of the organizations or those being hired.

What I do believe in is talent. And talent comes in all nationalities, ages, religions, and genders. So if your organization is dominated by a bunch of white males in their 50s, I don't think you're evil, but I do think you should consider broadening your hiring pool.

I've met several executives over the years who were interested in diversifying their workforces for one reason: avoiding discrimination litigation. Bad reasoning. Big picture leaders understand that talent comes in all shapes and sizes. The best leaders don't care what skin color someone has or what church he or she attends. The only thing that matters is whether or not they produce.

Corporate executives could learn from Raymond Heer, a long-time sailor, graduate of the Naval Academy, and currently the captain of a luxury yacht, the Andiamo. Heer has spent a good portion of his life leading extremely diverse crews on long voyages around the world. His current crew would make the United Nations proud. He employs men and women of different ages from Australia, New Zealand, England, South Africa, Mexico, and the Philippines. "The advantage of running a yacht in international waters is that I can choose my crew from every country in the world," says Heer. "That gives me a pool of 6.7 billion people."

The best leaders don't care what skin color someone has or what church he or she attends. The only thing that matters is whether or not they produce on the job.

Over the years, Heer has put together a yachting all-star team as he selects talented individuals from around the globe. For instance, Australia and New Zealand are known for producing top engineers, so that's where Heer goes to recruit. The Philippines is known for producing many of the best seamen and several Filipinos currently work for Captain Heer.

In addition to possessing specific technical skills, Heer believes a diverse crew provides a customer service advantage because guests on the Andiamo are different ages, from different backgrounds, and come from all over the world. Heer says there is always an employee who can "connect" or "share a joke" with the passengers. "Having an international crew with a broad background makes things much more interesting for the guests," says Heer.

Heer also believes that maintaining a diverse crew improves employee morale. "I try to keep the mix as varied as possible," he says. "If you have too many people from one culture, then there is the opportunity for them to associate only with each other and shun the others."

Obviously, if your company is in Des Moines, Iowa, or Wichita, Kansas, you don't have access to the same range of candidates as worldwide recruiter Heer. You can't hire your plant manager in one country and your line supervisors in another. However, Heer's overall philosophy on hiring remains valid. He believes in broadening your hiring pool as much as possible so that you can bring in a diverse group of talented individuals.

At the end of the day, you can look at diversifying your workforce in two ways. It's either an exercise in political correctness or it's an opportunity to select from a wider range of talented people of different ages, backgrounds, and nationalities.

Pay Employees What They're Worth When They're Worth It

"If you pay peanuts, you get monkeys."

- James Goldsmith

J ulie, a bright, talented 27-year-old sales associate, walks into her supervisor's office and politely hands him her letter of resignation. Julie is an up-and-coming star. She is smart, hardworking, and likable, the type of employee who forms the foundation of any good company. "I've really enjoyed working here," she says. "But I've received a significantly better offer from one of our competitors."

The boss studies the letter for a few seconds and ponders the situation, his ego clearly bruised. "How could she possibly want to leave? Why wouldn't she want to work for me?" he asks himself. Then he decides he's not going to lose one of his top employees to the competition and he coolly asks Julie, "So what's it going to cost for me to keep you?"

Blunders like these occur hundreds of times every day in the business world. Myopic bosses under-paying key employees and then scrambling to keep them after the competition has made them a better offer.

There's a simple solution for avoiding scenarios like this: Pay employees what they're worth, when they're worth it. If you've identified a star performer, don't wait until her annual review to give her a raise. Give it to her now.

"If you've got a terrific employee you've got to do everything to keep them," says Deb Kastelic, director of operations for North American Scientific. "If giving my best employees a few more dollars an hour is going to significantly increase my chances of keeping them, I would be crazy not to do that."

Ironically, the day I interviewed Kastelic, she had just given a raise to an unsuspecting lab technician who was her top performer. "It wasn't time for her review or for her annual raise, but I wanted to recognize her for the terrific work she was doing," says Kastelic. "So I found a way to get her a raise. I couldn't give her a ton of money because things are tight at the company, but if nothing else, I hope it shows her that I value her."

> "If giving my best employees a few more dollars an hour is going to significantly increase my chances of keeping them, I would be crazy not to do that."
>
> Deb Kastelic, Director of Operations
> North American Scientific

"We only review pay annually" is probably the most common excuse I hear from shortsighted bosses who insist upon shortchanging star employees. I don't buy it. If you have any savvy as a leader, you'll find a way around the arcane company policy and get a few more bucks for your high performer.

Another mistake I see poor managers make is to take it personally when one of their employees asks for a raise. I find this absurd, but all too often I see bosses take offense at the "disloyalty" of an employee who asks for a raise.

"That's not being realistic," says Kastelic. "First and foremost, employees are at work to provide for themselves and their families. It's ridiculous for managers to take a request for a raise personally. There's nothing wrong with employees asking for more money. And if the employee is doing exceptional work, you should try to get it for them."

Don't Throw the Annual Curve Ball

"Communication works for those who work at it."

- John Powell

Jack, a fifth-year attorney at a large Portland, Oregon law firm, walked into his annual performance review feeling pretty good about himself. Jack had billed a large number of hours during the course of the year and won two major trials for a couple of the firm's largest clients. As far as Jack knew, he would receive a stellar review and a nice pay raise. Instead, he walked unsuspectingly into a buzz saw.

As Jack entered the office of the senior partner he saw several bullet-pointed comments written in large black ink on a white board. Some examples included:

- February: "Opening statement during trial lacked passion and failed to engage the jury."

- May: "Did not appear well prepared for jury selection."

- August: "Legal brief for XYZ Corporation wordy and poorly organized."

- December: "Billable hours down for third month in a row."

"My boss had saved everything I had done wrong throughout the course of the year and hit me with it during my annual review," says Jack. "He didn't say a word to me about any of these mistakes all year and then he dumped them on me during my review. It felt more like a cross examination than a performance review."

The scenario I've described is all too common. A manager says nothing about performance for 12 months and then unloads on an employee during the annual review. In this instance, Jack's boss made several errors. First and foremost, he obviously viewed Jack's review as a once-a-year occasion to give feedback. Instead, he should have been providing Jack with feedback about his performance all year long.

Good managers actually deemphasize annual reviews. They view managing performance as an ongoing process instead of a one-time event.

Good leaders actually deemphasize annual reviews. They view managing performance as an ongoing process instead of a one-time event. If a leader does a good job of providing continuous performance feedback, the annual review should be a simple recap of what you've been discussing with the employee all year long.

Here are some additional suggestions for providing valuable performance feedback:

- **Provide specifics.** Telling an employee, "You're not working up to your potential" is not helpful. Instead, be specific about your expectations. For instance, say, "You're currently doing 60% of standard which is…."

- **Don't be belligerent.** Don't say, "Your work stinks and it's got to get better." Instead say, "Let's talk about what improvements need to be made in regards to your work performance."

- **Identify solutions.** It's not sufficient for a manager to point out the mistakes an employee makes. Don't say, "You have to hit your numbers." Try saying something like, "I have a couple of suggestions for improving your sales numbers including…"

In Jack's case, he eventually got so frustrated with the senior partner's management style that he left the firm. He is now a partner at a different Portland firm and has several young attorneys working for him. These days, he employs a significantly different approach when mentoring new lawyers.

"I talk to the people who work for me about their performance just about every day," he says. "I try to be respectful with them and, most importantly, I try not to surprise them during their yearly review."

Retain and Profit

"Great things are accomplished by talented people who believe they will

accomplish them."

- Warren G. Bennis

Gayle Blank figures he's built more than 3,000 miles of road and poured more than three million pounds of concrete in his 30-year career. Blank, a paving foreman for Idaho Sand and Gravel, is known as one of the best road builders in the Northwest and is a legend within the industry. He has vast industry knowledge and understands all the technical aspects of road building, but he's actually better known for a different skill set.

Blank is unique in the road-building business in that he has kept the same basic paving crew together for more than a decade in a business where turnover is often more than 300% annually. "I guess I must do something right," says Blank in his typical understated manner. "They keep coming back and giving the company a hard day of work."

Paving roads is physically taxing work, especially in the summer when temperatures soar well above 100 degrees. It's hard to retain employees for a week, let alone several years. Yet one of Blank's employees has been with him for 18 years, another 16, and two others for a decade. "If I had to recruit four new employees tomorrow, my job would be 500% more difficult," says Blank. "Having great employees makes my job easier, so why wouldn't I do everything I can to keep them?"

Blank insists he has no secret recipe for retaining employees. "I just listen to them and keep an eye on them. If they screw up, I don't get upset about it. You have to screw up to learn. I certainly have made my share of mistakes."

Blank also believes that loyalty only occurs when you recognize that employees have lives beyond the workplace. "I

> *"If I had to recruit four new employees tomorrow, my job would be 500% more difficult."*
>
> **Gayle Blank, Paving Foreman**
> **Idaho Sand and Gravel**

don't get over involved in employees' personal lives, but I know the names of their wives and children, and I try to know something about each of them personally. My employees also know if they have a crisis, I'll give them time off without asking a bunch of questions. I just tell them to go take care of things then I grab their shovel or get on their paver."

He probably wouldn't admit it, but Blank understands what most high-powered executives don't: People work for their manager, not their company. Show me a situation where good employees have stuck with an organization for more than a decade and I can guarantee you there's a good leader to be found. On the other hand, whenever I'm hired to consult for an organization where rampant turnover is the norm, I almost always find a micro-manager, a tyrant, or an egomaniac running the show.

"I've got a pretty basic approach," says Blank. "I let employees know how they're performing. Good or bad, I tell them how they're doing. Then I try to support them and compliment them when they do good work. There's nothing real fancy to the way I lead. Quite frankly, that's the only way I know how to be."

Don't Be Afraid to Cut Your Losses

"Executives owe it to the organization and to their fellow workers not to tolerate nonperforming individuals in important jobs."

- Peter Drucker

About half the time a company calls me for an "executive coaching" project, what I find is a complete train wreck. The client usually says something like, "We've got this employee who is really talented, but doesn't have very good people skills." Over the years, I've learned that saying someone "doesn't have good people skills" is actually code. What the client really means is, "He's sexually harassing half the staff and verbally abusing the rest," or "She's an egomaniac who has chased off most of her department."

Trying to "coach" one of these employees after he or she has created a wave of destruction is a little like doing marriage counseling when one person has already filed for divorce. Your chances of salvaging the situation are close to zero because simply too much damage has been done. Sometimes, it's better for an organization to cut its losses by terminating the employee and moving on.

There's an old adage in corporate circles: "Hire slowly and fire quickly." Yet few organizations actually practice what they preach. "Most companies are way too slow to terminate problem employees," says Pat Duncan, director of human resources for Gem State Manufacturing. "Some people are just really kind and want to try and save everyone. Other managers can't stand conflict so they resist making the tough discussions. But eventually, it can't be avoided."

Duncan, who has owned a small business of her own in addition to working for more than 20 years in human resources, looks for two things when trying to determine whether to salvage an employee. "If they've either given up or just don't care, you shouldn't try to save them," says Duncan, "On the other hand, when employees really care and will work hard to improve, I've found that they can be salvaged about 90% of the time."

> "Some people are just really kind and want to try to save everyone. Other managers can't stand conflict so they resist making the tough decisions."
>
> Pat Duncan, Director of Human Resources Gem State Manufacturing

Personally, I consider two basic principles when deciding whether to terminate an employee and I learned both in Psychology 101. The first is that the best predictor of future behavior is past behavior. If an employee has chronic behavioral or attendance problems, a written warning might improve things for a while, but chances are, the problems will return.

The second principle I consider when pondering whether to give a problem employee a pink slip is that skills can improve but personality typically doesn't change. So if you think the tyrannical sales manager can be coached into becoming a nice guy, you're kidding yourself. And if you're hoping the master manipulator down in Accounting can be turned into a team player, dream on. Go through the progressive discipline process and get these people out of your organization.

The consequences can be extremely ugly when companies fail to address problem employees in a timely manner. Litigation, low morale, and limited production are just a few of the likely consequences. "Managers usually know if they've made a disastrous hire within a few weeks, but it often takes us months or even years to get rid of problem employees," says Duncan. "The best managers recognize they've made a mistake and aren't afraid to cut their losses."

Part V

SIMPLE
MOTIVATIONAL
STRATEGIES

Identify What Motivates
Your Employees

"Management is nothing more than motivating other people."

- Lee Iacocca

Not every employee aspires to be a CEO. Some don't much like the thought of being a vice president either. Frankly, some very good employees get hives at the thought of managing hundreds of workers, reporting to the board of directors, or putting in the countless hours often required to succeed as an executive in the corporate world. Executives, who are often motivated by money and power, tend to mistakenly assume their employees are motivated by the same things.

The reality is that every employee is different and so is what motivates them.

Some employees prefer a flexible schedule to a fat paycheck. Some love to be praised publicly while others prefer a quiet pat on the back. New challenges motivate certain employees and others thrive in structured, traditional, predictable environments.

Countless studies have found praise or appreciation to be the number one motivator of employees. Financial reward usually ranks third or fourth, behind recognition, good leadership, and effective communication.

It's time to stop assuming and start asking your employees some basic questions. I'm often amazed when I find out that managers have gone years without asking their employees basic questions like, "What are your career goals?" and "What motivates you?"

Nancy Mueller, the founder of Nancy's Specialty Foods, was smart enough to ask a couple of these simple questions shortly after starting her company. As a result, she was able to hire and retain an employee who played a major role in her company's success.

> "My experience has been that many of the best employees are motivated by something besides money."
>
> Nancy Mueller, Founder
> Nancy's Specialty Foods

"I was just starting my business and looking for good employees," says Mueller, who turned her passion for making holiday hors d'oeuvres into a sixty million dollar a year business. "One day, in walked a really impressive woman named Erminia. She was intelligent, mature, and friendly, but she told me she only wanted to work for three months so she could make enough money to buy her daughter a wedding dress. Well, more than 12 years later, Erminia was still working for me...essentially acting as our operations manager."

So how did Mueller convince Erminia to stay 12 years longer than she had planned? "When I saw that she was going to be so terrific, I sat her down and talked to her about what was important to her in a job," says Mueller. "She said family was more important than work, but she said she would stay if she could do some things to create more of a family environment within the company. I told her to do it."

In the coming years Erminia, who is Hispanic, supervised ninety percent of the employees, who were also largely Spanish speaking. "She understood the backgrounds of the employees much better than I did so I allowed her to help create our corporate culture," says Mueller. "She basically became a mother figure to most of the employees and handled discipline, performance feedback, and just about everything else. This allowed me to focus on strategy."

Mueller says she compensated Erminia well, the strategy that most companies use to retain their top employees. However, Mueller is convinced that while additional pay probably didn't hurt, it wasn't the most important factor. "My experience has been that many of the best employees are motivated by something besides money and that was the case with Erminia. Relationships, a family-friendly environment, and a sense of team were more important to her. Fortunately, I took the time to ask her."

The best managers spend some time with their top employees discovering what motivates them. Once they've identified the motivators, good leaders are flexible enough to create an environment where their top employees can thrive.

Know Everybody's Name

"Sometimes when we are generous in small, undetectable ways it can change

someone's life forever."

- Margaret Cho

"**I**t drives me nuts when I can't remember a new employee's name," says Ryan DeLuca, the 29-year-old CEO of Bodybuilding.com. "These employees are working hard every day for my company, and the least I can do is know their names and a little bit about each of them."

Most people would probably excuse DeLuca for an occasional memory lapse. After all, Bodybuilding.com has gone from a few hundred dollars in sales to a 100-million dollar a year company in about eight years. DeLuca and his brother started the company in 1999 out of his garage. Now, he is responsible for more than 200 workers in multiple states.

Knowing employees' names is a good start, but it's just one piece of DeLuca's employee-friendly approach to leading. In fact, when you ask DeLuca the key to the company's success, he responds without pause. "It's been hiring and keeping good people. There's no question about it," he says. And what's DeLuca's secret to retaining his top performers? "I try and treat each one of them like individuals. I get to know them and I try and know their families as much as possible."

DeLuca is such a proponent of maintaining employee morale that he has removed himself from many of the day-to-day operations of Bodybuilding.com. Instead, he focuses most of his time on maintaining employee morale. "Taking care of the people and setting the strategy are my two main jobs," he says. "And even when faced with those two jobs, the people come first."

Some of DeLuca's employee recognition strategies are fairly common. For instance, he walks the floor of the warehouse each day complimenting his employees. He tries to be "specific" and "timely" with his praise so that employees know they're doing well.

> **"I try and treat each one of them (employees) like individuals. I get to know them and I try and know their families as much as possible."**
>
> Ryan DeLuca, CEO
> Bodybuilding.com

However, DeLuca also engages in some less conventional employee recognition practices. For instance, he takes at least one employee to lunch every week and asks that individual for feedback about the direction of the company. "I tell them they can comment on anything to do with the organization including pay, leadership, operations, anything," he says. "Obviously, at first they were a little hesitant to speak openly, but once people learn you're open to their ideas they begin to speak freely."

DeLuca also recognizes that while giving employees a pat on the back or allowing them to have input into the company are nice, it's also essential to recognize employees monetarily. Therefore, when DeLuca spots an employee providing exceptional customer service, working long hours, or demonstrating strong leadership skills, he has been known to give out $50 and $100 bonuses right on the spot.

However, even when the money is the reward, DeLuca distributes the funds with a personal touch. "I suppose I could just tell payroll to put a few extra dollars in an employee's check, he says. "But when I see someone doing something special, I want to shake their hand, call them by name, and thank them personally."

Get Over Yourself

"Life is a long lesson in humility."

- James Matthew Barrie

In his bestselling book, *Good to Great,* Jim Collins presents some of the most comprehensive research ever conducted on attributes of great leaders. What Collins found is that the two most important qualities a great leader can possess are drive and humility.

Based on my consulting experience, drive is something that just about all top executives possess. Humility is another story. In recent years, I have seen executives throw tantrums over the location of their parking spots, the size of their offices, the amount of administrative support they receive, and their job titles. And that's only for starters.

One person you won't find quibbling over executive privileges is Kathy Moore, CEO of West Valley Medical Center in Caldwell, Idaho. In fact, Moore, a five foot, one inch bundle of energy, is routinely teased by employees about how often she is seen picking up trash around the hospital. "Why wouldn't I pick up trash?" asks Moore, as she laughs about the good-natured ribbing from her colleagues. "I don't care what position I hold. I'm not going to walk by trash, a spill in the cafeteria, or a mess in a patient's room. If staff needs help, I'm going to help."

Moore's custodial duties actually represent a very small part of what she does each day. Obviously, her primary concerns are hospital strategy, finances, and patient satisfaction. However, Moore believes that picking up trash and cleaning an occasional bed pan are ways she can demonstrate to hospital employees that she is "no better or more important than anyone else."

Another way Moore demonstrates humility is by constantly communicating with employees at all levels of the organization. CEOs are often viewed by entry-level employees as aloof, but not Moore. In fact, Moore prides herself on "acknowledging every person I walk by the entire day," she says. "I don't care if it's an employee, a patient, or a visiting family member, I try to smile or say hello."

> **"I don't care if it's an employee, a patient, or a visiting family member, I try to smile or say hello."**
> **Kathy Moore, CEO**
> **West Valley Medical Center**

Some might think Moore is a little over the top in trying to communicate with everyone she encounters during the day, but she doesn't waiver when asked if she's over-communicating. "Walking the halls of the hospital is my opportunity to acknowledge people and thank them for working here or, if they are patients, letting them know we appreciate being able to serve them."

There are additional ways a leader can demonstrate humility. One is to take unconditional responsibility when things go wrong instead of pointing fingers at employees. Humble leaders also publicly praise employees for strong performance. Sadly, research in *Good to Great* actually found that managers often decline to compliment their high-performing employees, fearing one of those individuals may someday replace them. Meanwhile, humble managers coach employees, delegate responsibility, and prepare their successors.

Another way to demonstrate humility is to occasionally poke fun at yourself, something Moore does on a regular basis. Some of her favorite topics for self-deprecation include her height, her fashion sense, and how "touchy feely" she tends to be.

"I think any leader trying to portray herself as someone without flaws is making a mistake. I've got lots of flaws and I'm quite open about some of them. I hope that sends a message to employees that I'm not perfect and I certainly don't expect them to be."

Understand Your Audience

"If what you say is from your deepest feelings, you'll find an

audience that responds."

- Irwin Greenburg

Most churches in America are shrinking. Protestant, Catholic, you name the denomination and it's getting smaller. Some churches are losing as much as twenty percent of their membership annually. The primary reason for dwindling membership is that fewer young adults are going to church.

The question is, why?

"Ministers and priests aren't tailoring their messages to their audience," says Mike McClenahan, pastor at Solana Beach Presbyterian Church in the San Diego area. "Young people want to be inspired. They won't just blindly participate in something if they can't relate to it."

According to McClenahan, many church leaders continue to stand in the pulpit reading scripture and delivering sermons that have little meaning for many in the audience. "Thirty years ago this approach might have worked, but to communicate effectively you've got to continually evaluate who you're talking to, and how you send your message.'

McClenahan, who sold pharmaceuticals before leaving the corporate world for the church two decades ago, knows you must first get someone's attention before communicating effectively. "Whether you're trying to motivate employees in business or members in a congregation, you need to understand who you're talking to then deliver a message that is understandable and meaningful to them."

If you watch one of McClenahan's sermons you won't find him parked in the pulpit. He moves around the church talking, laughing, and telling stories like someone who has had a little too much caffeine. He talks about his marriage, his family, and everyday life challenges. "I take the scripture and relate the passages to stories about real life. My goal is to tell stories people can relate to."

"To communicate effectively you've got to continually evaluate who you're talking to and how you send your message."

Mike McClenahan, Pastor
Solana Beach Presbyterian Church

McClenahan's approach appears to be working. At a time when most churches are desperately trying to hang on to members, Solana Beach Presbyterian is growing. In McClenahan's six plus years as the pastor, membership has gone from 900 to 1,300.

McClenahan's simple communication strategies are certainly transferrable to the corporate world. Whenever communicating with a group of employees a leader should:

- **Consider the audience.** Are you communicating with executives or entry-level employees, sales people or accountants, older employees or younger?

- **Tailor the message.** Should your communication style be formal or conversational, humorous or serious, detailed or "big picture?"

- **Identify the goal.** Is it a brainstorming meeting or do you need the group to make a decision? Are you trying to educate your audience or motivate them?

"When you're trying to motivate and educate a group of people it's really up to the leader to figure out the best way to present his or her message," says McClenahan. "If you try the same approach with everyone it's probably not going to work. But if you try to understand your audience, you have a good chance of communicating your message successfully."

Say Thanks Every Day

"I can live for two months on a good compliment."

- Mark Twain

Over the years, I've heard a litany of excuses from bad managers who don't compliment their employees often enough. Here are some of my favorites:

- "I don't want them getting overconfident or they'll stop working hard."

- "They're just doing their jobs. That's what their pay-checks are for."

- "If you praise them too often, they'll start to expect it."

- "I don't need to be thanked, why do they?"

- "I like to keep them guessing."

- "My employees know that no news is good news."

These managers don't have a clue what they're talking about. The bottom line is that employees like to be recognized for a job well done. As for those macho "old school" types who say, "I don't need praise for doing my job," I say they're lying. In fact, in my experience, these are typically the first employees who whine about the company not recognizing their hard work.

Probably the most common argument against consistently praising employees is that the compliments will begin to lose their impact. I disagree. As long as a manager is specific about what the employee is doing well, the praise will be interpreted as genuine. For instance, if a supervisor says, "Great job, Jack," at the end of each work day, then chances are, it will start sounding fake. However, if the manager says, "Jack, I love the way you smiled and shook hands with that customer when you greeted him," the praise sounds genuine.

> **As long as a manager is specific about what the employee is doing well, the praise will be interpreted as genuine**

Here are a few other simple strategies for praising employees:

- **Praise in a timely manner.** Whenever possible, compliment employees right after they've performed the desired behavior. Don't wait until the end of the day and certainly don't wait until the next staff meeting. Praise employees for good work immediately and they are more likely to repeat the behavior.

- **Praise new employees frequently.** I don't know about you, but two weeks into every job I've ever had I thought I might get fired. I didn't understand the computer system, couldn't send a fax, and felt totally incompetent and insecure. These early days are the times when new employees really need to be reassured.

Look for opportunities to praise them and reassure them they're doing well.

- **Get creative with your compliments.** I've seen managers come up with some pretty original ways of thanking their employees over the years and usually their creativity pays off. One manager sent thank you letters to employees' homes. And, in addition to thanking the employee, he thanked spouses for their understanding and sacrifice to the organization. Another supervisor routinely wrote up employees for "performance excellence." Most employees only get written up when they've done something wrong, but this supervisor would also do write-ups for exceptional performance. He would simply jot down three or four sentences describing the employee's positive behavior, put one copy in the personnel file, and give another copy to the employee.

Charles Schwab, a giant in the financial world and someone known for going to great lengths to recognize employees, is a leader who understands the importance of showing appreciation. He says, "I have yet to find a person who did not do better work under a spirit of approval than under a spirit of criticism."

I believe that employees will forgive you many of your failings (disorganization, personality quirks, etc.) as long as you consistently demonstrate appreciation for their hard work. Don't ever withhold praise from employees when they do good work. If you don't get anything else right as a manager, get that right.

Leadership Isn't Rocket Science (Interviewees)

- Special thanks to all of the great leaders who shared their time, knowledge and experience so that I could write this book.

Don Bailey, CEO ....Questcor Pharmaceuticals

Gayle Blank, Paving Foreman..Idaho Sand and Gravel

Renee Bobrowski, MD ....Saint Alphonsus Medical Group

Linda Chandler, Store Manager ....WinCo Foods

Tabb Compton, Sales Manager ....Crucial Technology

Ryan DeLuca, CEO ....Bodybuilding.com

Pat Duncan, Director of Human Resources............Gem State Manufacturing

Bob Dyson, Owner ....Napa Auto Parts

Raymond Heer ....Yacht Captain

Greg Jordan, Managing Partner ....Reed Smith Law Firm

Deb Kastelic, Director of Operations ....North American Scientific

George Kotch, Global Crop Leader ....Syngenta Seeds

Angela Lewton ....High Tech Executive

Bill Long, Chairman of the Board..WinCo Foods

Mike McClenahan, Pastor ....Solana Beach Presbyterian Church

Matt McCormick, Director of Sales ....Peet's Coffee

Kathy Moore, CEO ....West Valley Medical Center

Jennifer Miller,

   Director of Human Resources ....Electronic Controls Corporation

Nancy Mueller, Founder ....Nancy's Specialty Foods

Michael Roach, M.D. ....Saint Alphonsus Medical Group

John Sears, Plant Manager ....Smoke Guard Smoke Systems

Faye Wattleton, President ....Center for Advancement of Women

About the Author

Grant is the founder of Thompson Consulting Group (TCG), a management consulting company that focuses on leadership development. Grant is a popular speaker and well-respected executive coach. He has coached and trained thousands of leaders in dozens of industries across the United States. Grant is known for his easygoing consulting style and practical, straightforward advice. Prior to becoming a consultant, Grant worked as corporate executive, teacher and broadcast journalist. Grant has a Doctorate in Psychology, a Masters Degree from the University of San Francisco's School of Education and a Bachelor's Degree in Communications from the University of Southern California. Grant lives in Boise, Idaho with his wife and three children. Find out more about Grant and TCG at www.thompsonconsulting.com.